Anonymus

Summer Homes among the Mountains

Anonymus

Summer Homes among the Mountains

ISBN/EAN: 9783743344822

Manufactured in Europe, USA, Canada, Australia, Japa

Cover: Foto ©ninafisch / pixelio.de

Manufactured and distributed by brebook publishing software
(www.brebook.com)

Anonymus

Summer Homes among the Mountains

Summer Homes

IN THE

BERKSHIRE AND
LITCHFIELD HILLS

WELCOME

ISSUED BY THE

Philadelphia · Reading & New England R.R.

THE FOWLER & MILLER COMPANY,
PRINTERS AND BINDERS,
341 MAIN ST., HARTFORD, CONN.

Summer Homes

AMONG THE MOUNTAINS

ON THE

Philadelphia, Reading & New England R. R.

POUGHKEEPSIE BRIDGE ROUTE.

TICKETS AND TIME TABLES CAN BE PROCURED AT ANY OF THE
OFFICES OF

WESTCOTT'S EXPRESS,

NEW YORK TRANSFER CO. (Dodd's Express),

NEW YORK CENTRAL & HUDSON RIVER R. R.,

HUDSON RIVER DAY LINE,

NEW YORK, ONTARIO & WESTERN RAILWAY
IN
NEW YORK CITY AND BROOKLYN.

J K. O. SHERWOOD, Receiver,
192 Broadway, New York.

C. M. LAWLER, Gen'l Manager.
Hartford, Conn.

W. J. MARTIN, Gen'l Passenger Agent,
Hartford, Conn.

HOW TO REACH RESORTS ON THIS LINE. RATES OF FARE, AND APPROXIMATE SUMMER TIME-TABLE.

TRAINS TO NEW YORK.

STATIONS.	Mond'y Sp'l.	Berks. Exp.	St'mb't Exp.	Day Exp.	Sunday only
NEW YORK—N. Y., O. & W.			P.M. 6.00	P.M. 7.25	P.M. 9.35
" " Day Line					P.M. 7.25
" " Harlem Div N. Y. C.		A.M. 11.50		4.45	
CAMPBELL HALL				4.25	7.15
EAST WALDEN				4.04	6.25
MODENA				3.41	6.29
CLINTONDALE				3.34	6.12
LLOYD				3.26	4.67
HIGHLAND				3.17	4.00
POUGHKEEPSIE				3.10	5.32
HIBERNIA				2.42	5.25
STANFORDVILLE				2.31	5.11
PINE PLAINS				2.03	4.82
RHINECLIFF			12.25	1.53	
ANCRAM			11.20	1.84	1.25
COPAKE			11.08	1.20	1.12
BOSTON CORNERS			11.02	1.20	4.07
MT. RIGA					
MILLERTON		9.05	10.12	1.06	3.50
LAKEVILLE		8.35	10.39	1.02	3.46
SALISBURY	A.	8.07	10.23	12.45	3.23
CANAAN					3.00
NORFOLK		7.45	10.03	12.11	10.39
WINSTED		7.20	9.40	11.42	10.09
NEW HARTFORD		A.M.	9.22	11.29	9.54
COLLINSVILLE			9.08	11.09	9.39
SIMSBURY			8.45	10.45	9.16
HARTFORD			8.16	10.15	8.40
SPRINGFIELD			7.00	7.50	7.30
BOSTON—B. & A.			A.M.	A.M.	A.M.

TRAINS FROM NEW YORK.

STATIONS.	Sunday only	Berks. Exp.	St'mb't Exp.	Day Exp.
NEW YORK—N. Y., O. & W.	A.M. E.9.15		A.M. 8.40	A.M. 7.35
" " Day Line		P.M. 8.40		9.04
" " Harlem Div N. Y. C.				
CAMPBELL HALL	9.15			10.15
EAST WALDEN	P.M. 12.16			10.34
MODENA	12.32			10.53
CLINTONDALE	12.55			11.04
LLOYD	1.07		P.M.	11.10
HIGHLAND	1.12		2.20	11.12
POUGHKEEPSIE	1.26		2.29	11.25
HIBERNIA	1.55		2.59	11.47
STANFORDVILLE	2.07		3.18	11.57
PINE PLAINS	2.38			12.16
RHINECLIFF				12.30
ANCRAM	2.43		4.08	12.46
COPAKE	2.53		4.12	12.55
BOSTON CORNERS	3.03	6.22	4.30	1.06
MT. RIGA				1.21
MILLERTON	3.27	6.33	4.50	1.41
LAKEVILLE	3.30	6.35		1.47
SALISBURY	3.35	6.55	5.21	2.12
CANAAN				
NORFOLK	4.22	7.15	5.36	2.38
WINSTED	4.49	7.49		2.45
NEW HARTFORD	5.06	P.M.	5.36	3.29
COLLINSVILLE	5.26		5.97	3.57
SIMSBURY	5.32		6.66	4.09
HARTFORD	6.30		6.49	4.30
SPRINGFIELD	7.27		7.27	5.40
BOSTON—B. & A.	10.00		10.00	9.25
	P.M.		P.M.	P.M.

RATES OF FARE.

STATIONS.	Via N. Y., O. & W. Ry. via C. Hall.	Hudson River Day Line via Rhinecliff.	N. Y. C. Harlem Div.	From Hartford.
CAMPBELL HALL	$1.56			$3.74
EAST WALDEN	1.83			3.47
MODENA	2.07			3.23
CLINTONDALE	2.22			3.11
LLOYD	2.22			3.02
HIGHLAND	2.36			2.90
POUGHKEEPSIE				2.75
HIBERNIA				2.45
STANFORDVILLE				2.73
PINE PLAINS		$1.25		2.73
RHINECLIFF		2.03		3.30
ANCRAM		2.21		2.52
COPAKE		2.35		2.31
BOSTON CORNERS				2.22
MT. RIGA				2.18
MILLERTON		2.50	$2.65	2.07
LAKEVILLE		2.55	2.65	1.92
SALISBURY		2.65	2.61	1.89
CANAAN				1.65
NORFOLK		2.70	2.70	1.35
WINSTED		2.70	2.70	1.09
NEW HARTFORD		2.70		.87
COLLINSVILLE		2.70		.72
SIMSBURY		2.70		.45

E. via Erie R. R.

☞ Excursion Tickets, good for the season, are also on sale at all offices in New York City at reduced rates.

INTRODUCTION.

THE Philadelphia, Reading & New England Railroad
(Poughkeepsie Bridge route), extends from Campbell Hall, Orange County, New York, to Hartford,
Connecticut, a distance of 145 miles, with branches from
Poughkeepsie to Hopewell, New York, where connections
are made with the New York & New England and Newburgh, Dutchess & Connecticut Railroads, and from Silvernail, New York, to Rhinecliff, New York, where connections
are made with the New York Central & Hudson River Railroad and Hudson River steamboats. Starting from Campbell Hall the road runs due east through the rich farming
and fruit-producing section of Orange and Ulster Counties.
After one hour's ride Highland is reached, on the west
bank of the Hudson River. Here we approach the west end
of the great Poughkeepsie Bridge (which will be found fully
described elsewhere), spanning the American Rhine as the
rainbow. The views from the car windows as the traveler
crosses the bridge are the grandest to be seen from any railroad line in the world. Over the bridge we pass through
the beautiful hillside city of Poughkeepsie, thence through
Dutchess and Columbia Counties, where many summer
boarders are entertained. Reaching Boston Corners the road
crosses the Harlem Division of the New York Central &
Hudson River Railroad. At this point are the three States'
corners, and the place will long be remembered as the battle-
ground of the famous prize fight between "Yankee" Sullivan and Morrissey. At Millerton, a few miles beyond, we
make another connection with the Harlem Railroad. Here
through first-class coaches from the Grand Central Depot,

3

New York, are coupled to our train, conveying summer boarders with speed and comfort to the Berkshire and Litchfield hill resorts. Passing on our journey three miles distant the roadway skirts the shores of the beautiful lake at Lakeville, so justly noted for its pure, clear waters. It was here that the chain was made in revolutionary days and stretched across the Hudson below Newburgh, to prevent English war ships passing up that river. From this point we begin to climb the Berkshire and Litchfield hills, between whose lofty heights of living green, mystic purple, and dimmish blue lies an infinity of deep-rent ravines of icy waters and smiling valleys, lakes, and rivers.

Here, gentle reader, where heaven and earth meet, may be found the ideal summer home.

> There's a ripple of fountains
> That rise in the mountains,
>   And a murmur of rills
>   That spring in the hills,
> And the streams go on with a softer flow,
> And the sun goes down with a warmer glow,
> There's a smiling spot by the grand old mill
> In the dear old land of Litchfield Hill.

Passing on a few miles we reach the already noted summer resorts of Salisbury, Chapinville, Twin Lakes, Canaan, and Norfolk. Here we reach the apex and follow the descending grade through a picturesque country dotted with lakes and streams well stocked with game and fish, and next reach Winsted, a prosperous town surrounded by hills, which boasts of 7,000 inhabitants, unequaled water works, besides a beautiful lake and fine drives.

Next we reach New Hartford, beautifully situated, with thriving factories and summer attractions. At Collinsville we cross the Farmington River, noted for its excellent bass fishing and pretty village. Passing on we reach Simsbury and Tariffville, with charming mountain and river scenery. Passing Bloomfield we end our journey at Hartford, the capital of the " Nutmeg State."

POUGHKEEPSIE BRIDGE.

"Bathed in the tenderest purple of distance,
Tinted and shadowed by pencils of air."

"SWEET HOME" has its joys, its endearments and its ties, but there comes a time to all of us when the yearning for change of scene and occupation overcomes even the affection we cherish for our "ain fireside." This desire to be up and away, to leave behind the carking cares of business and the wearing worries of every-day life, and to breathe a new air and look upon new scenes, usually recurs at that season when all out-of-doors is at its best; when the sun-kissed hill-tops beckon us to breezy heights, and the shadowed valleys woo us to repose; when the forest's mystic murmurings invite us to its cool, green gloom, and the plashing streams make music as they sing along their pebbly bed.

For the gratification of this annually recurring desire for rest and recreation, almost limitless facilities are at hand, so situated with reference to the crowded centers of population as to be conveniently accessible, and so varied in character as to please the greatest diversity of mood and liking.

Along the line of the Philadelphia, Reading & New England Railroad, and adjacent thereto, are some of the most delightful summer retreats in America. The Catskill Mountains, the Berkshire and Litchfield Hills, the valleys of the Hudson, the Wallkill, and the Connecticut Rivers, all are penetrated or reached by this railway and its immediate connections, while it is also a favorite tourists' route to the White Mountains and the many seacoast health and pleasure places of New England.

In the pages which follow will be found brief and general descriptive sketches of such localities as offer attractions to those in quest of summer homes, together with information respecting the accommodations obtainable, the special advantages claimed, and the rates charged for board.

6

"THE HILLHURST," A. E. McLEAN, PROPRIETOR, NORFOLK, CONN.

Let us enter upon our journey of exploration at the western terminus of the Philadelphia, Reading & New England, Campbell Hall, thirty miles to the sunsetward of the noble and historic Hudson. This is the point of connection with several important lines of railway; the main line of the New York, Ontario & Western Railroad, the Wallkill Valley Railroad, and the Erie lines. Leaving New York via the Ontario & Western 7.35 A. M. from Franklin Street and 7.50 from West 42d Street, connection will be made at Campbell Hall with the eastern express direct to all resorts reached by this line.

CAMPBELL HALL, ORANGE CO., N. Y.

Here is a pleasant village, set amid the broad and fertile farm lands of famous Orange County, where thrift and plenty walk hand in hand, and where the tired city dwellers will not seek in vain for the great *desiderata* of a vacation outing, quietude, and rest.

CAMPBELL HALL STATION — Campbell Hall Post Office.

MRS S. S. HALL — Boarding house. One quarter of a mile. Accommodates 15. Terms on application. Large piazza, plenty of shade, piano, croquet grounds, tennis, etc. Refers to Dr. D. G. Lippincott, Campbell Hall, N. Y.

EAST WALDEN, ORANGE CO., N. Y.

Walden is a pretty and enterprising village near the northern boundary line of Orange County. It has a population of three thousand, with Episcopalian, Methodist, and Dutch Reform Churches, as well as excellent preparatory and high schools. The surroundings are of a refreshingly pastoral character, while in the distance are visible the higher peaks of the Catskills.

8

FLOWER GARDEN, LAKE MOHONK, N. Y.

Many New York City people make their homes here, and there is no lack of agreeable society. By reason of its healthfulness it is gaining wide popularity as a summer resort. There is fair fishing in the Wallkill River. A number of families in the village and its vicinity receive boarders.

EAST WALDEN STATION — East Walden Post Office.

CHARLES E. WHIGAN — Farm House. One mile. Accommodates 40. Adults, $7; children, $5; transients, $2 per day. Private conveyance from station, no charge. Raises own vegetables. Pleasant surroundings. Convenient to churches. First-class livery. Discount for season guests. Refers to B. D. Pershall, 369 Third Avenue, New York City.

R. W. CORSA — Farm house. Half mile. Accommodates 10. Adults, $6; children, $4. Will meet guests at station without charge.

ST. ELMO, ORANGE CO., N. Y.

Located on the Borden Farm, near the great Borden Condensed Milk Factory, in a perfectly healthy and rich farming section, noted for its excellent fruit. Over 150 tons of grapes were shipped to the market from this station last season.

MODENA, ULSTER CO., N. Y.

Passing St. Elmo, near the pretty village of Wallkill, we come to Modena, Ulster County, occupying an elevated situation in the Wallkill Valley, with a fine view of the Shawangunk Mountains in the distance. It is in the midst of a region celebrated for the production of grapes and small fruits. The neighborhood is notably healthful, and many city people summer in and about this place.

MODENA STATION — Modena Post Office.

MRS. GEORGE ACKERMAN—Boarding house. Two miles. Accommodates 10. Adults, $5 to $6 per week; children, $4 to $5; transients, $2 per day. Will meet guests at station. Raises own vegetables. Good fishing in the Wallkill River near by. House has lovely shade around it and large lawn. Croquet and other amusements. Large, airy rooms.

H. MINARD — Farm house. Two miles. Accommodates 25. Adults, $5 to $8 ; reduction for children ; transients, $1.25 per day. Discount for season guests. Raises own vegetables, fruit, and berries. Pickerel fishing in lake near by, and Wallkill River boating and bathing. Carriage free from station for guests. House is beautifully situated, surrounded by large, shady lawn on an elevated table land 1,200 feet above tidewater, commanding a grand view of surrounding country. Refers to C. H. Sibbald, 387 Halsey Street, Brooklyn ; Drs. Moshier and Hall, 181 Joralemon Street, Brooklyn ; J. Barton, 307 East Nineteenth Street, New York ; S. McCullom, 13 Belmont Avenue, Jersey City, N. J.; Dr. A. Birdsall, 1,036 Bedford Avenue, Brooklyn, and many others.

ABRAHAM LINDERBECK — Farm house. One-half mile. Accommodates 10. Adults, $6 ; children, half price ; transients, $2 per day. Guests transported from station free of charge. Table supplied with fresh eggs, milk, and vegetables from our farm. Splendid views of Shawangunk Mountains, fine walks and drives. Every attention given to the comfort of guests.

MRS. A. P. LIMEBURNER — "Limeburner Villa." At station. Accommodates 25. Adults, $6 to $8 ; children, $3 to $4 ; transients, $1 to $1.25 per day. Discount for season guests. Large and attractive house and grounds. Hammocks, croquet and all kinds of games. Shady grounds, pleasant surroundings. Refers to Dr. C. A. Limeburner, Greenville, N. J., and others on application.

FRANK LANE — "Pine Hill Cottage." One mile. Accommodates 25. Adults, $5 to $6 ; reduction for children ; transients, $1 per day. Discount for season guests. Will meet guests at station with carriage ; no charge. Table liberally supplied with all farm products. Fine walks and drives. Will endeavor to please.

MRS. JAMES DWYER — "Wood Villa Farm." One mile. Accommodates 15. Adults, $5 ; children, $3 ; transients, $1 per day. Carriage will meet guests at station ; no charge. Table supplied with farm products. Bass and pickerel fishing in the vicinity. Pleasant surroundings, home comforts.

D. W. HASBROUCK — Wallkill Post Office. Boarding house. Accommodates 40. $6 per week. Full particulars upon application.

JAMES H. COUTANT — Ardonia, Ulster County, N. Y. Farm house. Two miles. Accommodates 20. Adults, $6 ; children, $4 ; transients, $1 per day. Table liberally supplied with farm products. This house is pleasantly situated, grounds well shaded. Fine walks and drives. Excellent water, healthy location. Refers to E. H. Colyer, Broad Street, Newark, N. J.; W. P. Underhill, 338 Broadway, New York ; Dr. E. H. Gerow, Poughkeepsie, N. Y.

E. L. SCHOONMAKER — New Hurley post office. Farm house. Three miles. Accommodates 13. $6 to $9 for adults, $4 for children ; transients, $1.75 per day. Conveyance will meet passengers at station ; charge, 25 cents. This house is a large two-story structure, with large piazza on two sides, standing on high ground, commanding beautiful scenery, and is considered a very healthy situation.

J. E. BROWN — Leptondale post office. Farm house. Five miles. Accommodates 12. Adults, $6 ; children at a reduction ; transients, $1 per day. Will meet guests at station with private conveyance ; no charge. Table liberally supplied with buttermilk and eggs, vegetables, and farm products. Lake and river fishing near by. Pleasant rooms and surroundings. Shady lawns, piazza ; excellent water. Christian home (Friends).

11

MRS. E. R. BARTLETT   Plattekill post office.   Three miles.   Farm house. Accommodates 15.   Adults, $6 to $7; children, $3; transients, $1.50 per day.   Carriage will meet guests at station; charge, 50 cents.   Table liberally supplied with farm products.   Fine piazza and plenty of shade.   For references and other particulars, apply.

FRANCIS GARRISON — Plattekill post office.   Farm house.   Four and one-half miles.   Accommodates 30 to 40.   Adults, $6; children at a reduction; transients, $1 per day.   Table supplied with farm products.   Fishing in Orange Lake.   Gunning, small game.   Refers to James Garrison, 76th Street and Park Avenue, New York City.

CLINTONDALE, ULSTER CO., N. Y.

This handsome village of Ulster County occupies a commanding site on the western slope of a range of hills overlooking the beautiful and fertile Wallkill Valley. In the background the rounded peaks of the Shawangunk Range loom against the sky.   In every direction the outlook is magnificent.   A further and very essential advantage is the unquestionable healthfulness of the locality.   In the vicinity there are excellent gunning and fishing.   Churches of several denominations are within convenient distance.

CLINTONDALE STATION — Clintondale Post Office.

MRS. S. P. THORN — Farm house.   Three-fourths mile.   Accommodates 45. $7 to $9 for adults; $5 to $6 for children.   Transients, $1.50 per day.   House is pleasantly situated.   Large, airy rooms.   Table liberally supplied with vegetables and other products from our own farm.   Bass and pickerel fishing in Wallkill river near by.   Livery accommodations.   One-fourth mile from church.   Write for further particulars.

JOHN W. WEAVER — Mountain View farm house.   One mile.   Accommodates 20. $6 per week for adults; reduction for children.   House is beautifully situated, commanding an extensive view of the Shawangunk Mountains, also of the Catskills. Hotels at these points can be seen thirty miles away.   Mountain side near by, where guests can enjoy the forest and extensive views.   Swings, rustic seats, summer-house, hammocks, etc.   Always plenty of milk furnished from our Jersey dairy; eggs, vegetables and farm products furnished in abundance.   Quiet, Christian home.   Refers to W. C. Tabor of Warner Publishing Co., 70 Warren Street, New York; Orlando Marine, Potter Building, New York; Charles Hall, 587 Lafayette Avenue, Brooklyn, and Miss Claribel Jeffrey, Park Conservatory, Newark, New Jersey.

E. S. ANDREWS — Boarding house.   One and one-half miles.   Accommodates 20.   Adults, $5 to $6 per week; transients, $1 per day.   Free carriage to and from station.   Discount to season guests.   Serve vegetables raised in our own garden. Good fishing in neighboring ponds; free boat for guests on Hurd's pond.   Livery on the place; excellent drives to numerous points of interest in vicinity.   Views from house are grand and extensive   No malaria nor mosquitoes.   Large, shady grounds. Fruit in abundance.   References on application.

12

SOLID COMFORT.

MRS. O. T. DINGEE — Mountain View Cottage. Near station. Accommodates 25. Terms. $5 to $6 per week. Bountiful table. Fine walks and drives. Numerous summer attractions. For further particulars and references apply.

MRS LAURA L. H. RUE — Farm house. Three-fourths mile. Accommodates 8. $6 to $7 per week ; children, $5. Transients, $1.25 per day. Raises own vegetables. Bass and pickerel fishing in Wallkill River near by. Gunning—partridge, quail, and rabbits. Abundance of shade. Pleasantly located grounds ; spring water, plenty of fruit. Post and telegraph office near by. Refers to Mr. and Mrs. J. N. Van Vliet, 318 West 129th Street, New York, and F. L. Dascher, 217 Ross Street, Brooklyn.

MRS. E. ELLIS — Farm house. Near station. Accommodates 10. Rates, $5 to $6 ; children, $3. Pleasant surroundings. Convenient to post and telegraph office. Romantic walks and drives. Perfectly healthy location.

W. R. BENEDICT — Leptondale post office. Farm house. Three miles. Accommodates 15. Adults, $5 to $6 ; children, half price ; transients, $1.50 per day. Carriage will meet guests at station, free. Vegetables from our own garden. Bass and pickerel fishing in Orange lake near by. Beautiful scenery for twenty miles in every direction. For full particulars write.

LOYD, ULSTER CO., N. Y.

This pleasant little hamlet is beautifully situated on the highlands of the Hudson, six miles west of Poughkeepsie, and the point where the Highland and New Paltz Electric Railroad crosses : here change cars for New Paltz and Lake Mohonk, and Minnewaska.

LOYD STATION — Loyd Post Office.

D. B. CARROLL — Farm house. One mile. Accommodates 15. Rates, $5 to $7 ; children, half price ; transients, $1 per day. Large, airy rooms. Shady lawn, good water, all conveniences. Free transportation from station. Raises own vegetables. Fishing and gunning.

S. P. CHAMPLIN — Farm house. Half mile. Accommodates 10. $6 per week. Children not taken. Discount for season guests. Raises own vegetables. Bass and pickerel fishing. Half mile from church. Good livery accommodations. Refers to L. Lane, postmaster.

D. M. SUTTON — Private residence. At station. Accommodates 6 to 8. Adults, $6 ; transients, $1 per day. Discount for season guests. Fishing and gunning. Good livery accommodations. Quarter of a mile from church.

A. K. SMILEY — Mohonk Lake, Ulster County, N. Y. Ten miles. Accommodates 400. $15 to $30 per week. Transients, $4 per day, June 25th to September 15th, $3 per day before and after. Stage meets passengers on notice ; transportation, $1.75. Boating. Excellent livery accommodations. Church service held in hotel. Write for circular. See description in book.

J. IRVING GODDARD — Mohonk Lake. Boarding house. Eight miles. Accommodates 36. $10 to $15 per week. Transients, $2 per day. Will meet guests at station when requested. Raises vegetables Beautiful scenery, summer attractions.

A. H. SMILEY—Minnewaska, Ulster County, N. Y. Accommodates 250. Terms and particulars upon application. See description elsewhere.

I. S. DAYTON — Ohioville post office. Farm boarding house. Two miles. Accommodates 15. $5 to $7 per week ; children half price. Transients, $1.50 per day. House situated on New Paltz turnpike, surrounded by pine and maple grove and lawn. Perfectly healthy location. Good conveyance for pleasure riding. Piano, croquet and dancing.

MRS. W. J. TALLMAN — Ohioville post office. Farm boarding house. Accommodates 14. $6 to $7 per week ; children half price. Full particulars on application.

LAKE MOHONK, LAKE MINNEWASKA, MOUNT MEENAHGA.

These are summer resorts of wide celebrity, reached by electric lines from Loyd Station. Their popularity increases each year, particularly since this line of railway has rendered them so easily accessible.

The Shawangunk Mountains, a partially detached portion of the great Appalachian chain, are a small range extending through Ulster County. At their northern extremity, a few miles west of the Hudson River, Sky-Top Peak looms high above the neighboring mountains. Near the summit of Sky-Top, one thousand two hundred feet above the level of the valley, is Lake Mohonk, a lovely sheet of water about three-quarters of a mile in length, clear as crystal, and bordered by massive rock formations and towering cliffs. The views in all directions are of great extent and indescribable grandeur, embracing large portions of six States, and covering several thousand square miles; "an outlook over two perfect valleys, with fifty miles of the western horizon crowded with glorious mountain ranges, amid whose mysterious realms the sinking sun and the mountain mists work such magic as only poetry exalted to worship can fitly rehearse."

The Lake Mohonk House, with a capacity of five hundred guests, is located on the edge of the lake, and commands a magnificent view of lake and mountain. Albert K. Smiley is the proprietor; his post-office address is Mohonk Lake, N. Y., and he will upon application send circulars containing full description of the house, terms, references, etc.

Lake Minnewaska, reached by a short stage-coach ride from Loyd Station, is on the summit of the Shawangunk Mountains, about five miles from Lake Mohonk, and is much larger than the latter. On two sides it is flanked by bold, precipitous cliffs, and on the other sides by sloping, wooded shores. The towering bluffs; the rugged masses of tumbled, massive boulders; the rich foliage of trees that spring from crevices in the rocks at the most surprising angles and inaccessible heights,— form a picture that the liveliest imagination cannot parallel.

The Minnewaska Mountain House is a very extensive establishment, situated upon Minnewaska Heights, one hundred and fifty feet above the lake, and eighteen hundred feet above tide-level. It is an excellent house in all respects, and is conducted by Alfred H. Smiley, whose post-office address is Minnewaska, N. Y., and who will promptly reply to inquiries relative to rooms, terms, etc.

HIGHLAND, ULSTER CO., N. Y.

Near the western bank of the Hudson, this pretty place, ensconced among the hills, has many advantages to commend it to the seeker for summer rest. There are many miles of pleasant drives, beautiful scenery, excellent boating facilities, and moderately good fishing.

HIGHLAND STATION — Highland Post Office.

A. C. HASBROUCK — Summer boarding house. One-eighth of a mile. Accommodates 20. $7 to $10 per week for adults ; children half price. House has double veranda, plenty of shade trees, large lawn. Fishing and gunning. Convenient to churches, livery, etc.

A. E. HASBROUCK — Bellevue Villa. Summer boarding house. One and one-quarter miles. Transportation by stage, 25 cents. Accommodates 90. $8 to $16 per week, children half price ; transients, $2 per day. Discount for season guests. For full particulars, write for circular.

LAKE MOHONK HOUSE.

CROSSING THE GREAT BRIDGE.

NEW ENGLAND'S NEW GATEWAY—POUGH-KEEPSIE BRIDGE.

This wonderful structure can rightfully be classed as one of the wonders of the world. Built entirely of steel, on great stone piers, it will last forever. The great bridge over the Firth of Forth in Scotland is larger, but next to this the Poughkeepsie Bridge is the largest in the world. The eastern viaduct alone is over one-half a mile in length, with twenty-four spans, the greatest being 175 feet long and 200 feet high. There are six main piers: No 1, located on the west shore of the Hudson: Nos. 2, 3, 4, and 5 in the Hudson River itself, and No. 6 on the east shore. There are two anchorages of masonry, 128 "Poney Piers," 36 being on the west side, and 92 on the east, forming foundations of the viaduct, and two abutments at the ends of the viaducts. Each of the main piers carries a steel tower 100 feet high, firmly braced and bolted to the masonry, and upon these towers rest the trusses and cantilevers of the superstructure (see illustration). The distance from shore to shore is 2,608 feet, and from center to center of shore piers 2,692 feet, covered by five principal spans, two of 548 feet long, one of 546, and two of 525. These latter are rectangular trusses, 130 feet in clear height above high water, and 82 feet from the bottom of the lower cord to the top of floor system, making the base of the rail 212 feet above high water. The length of the main bridge from anchorages is 3,093 feet 9 inches: that of the western viaduct, 1,033 feet 6 inches, and of the eastern viaduct, 2,640 feet; making the whole structure 6,767 feet 3 inches long. Over this runs a double track railway with a foot-path on each side. It is capable of sustaining at any given point two 85-ton engines, each drawing a train of 3,000 pounds weight per running

foot. The foundations contain 12,000,000 feet of timber, 40,000 cubic yards of concrete, and the piers about 20,000 cubic feet of masonry. The superstructure of the main bridge contains over 15,000 tons of mild open-hearth steel, and the viaducts over 6,000 tons of iron. The views north and south, from the car windows in passing over this bridge, are the grandest to be seen from any railroad line in the world. For miles the eye can sweep the horizon; twenty miles up or down the Hudson can be seen with the naked eye, and the view is beautiful and grand.

POUGHKEEPSIE, DUTCHESS CO., N. Y.

This is a handsome city of twenty-five thousand inhabitants, on the left bank of the Hudson, and elevated one hundred or two hundred feet above the river, while behind it rises College Hill, some three hundred feet in height. Its regularly laid out streets are shaded by fine old trees and bordered with handsome residences and prosperous business houses. It is the most important city between New York and Albany, and one of the most ancient, having been settled in 1698. It is a remarkably healthy, pleasant place of residence, combining the advantages of an elevated situation, pure air and water, with the immediate presence of all the comforts and conveniences of city life. Poughkeepsie enjoys a special reputation for its educational facilities. The famous Vassar College, the greatest female educational institution in the world, is just east of the city limits. Within the city are an opera house, free public library, and churches of all denominations.

POUGHKEEPSIE STATION — Poughkeepsie Post Office.

JAMES C. GRIGGS — Morgan House Hotel. Three-quarters of a mile. Accommodates 100. Rates : For adults, $2.50 to $3 per day ; half rates for children; discount for season guests. Hotel is first-class in every respect and finely situated.

H. N. BAIN — Nelson House Hotel. Three-quarters of a mile. Accommodates 250. $10 to $20 per week. This hotel is first-class in every respect, elegantly furnished. Sample rooms and every convenience,

20

MRS. WILLIAM BOGARDUS — Boarding house, Market Street. One mile
Accommodates 15. Rates $6 to $15 per week. First-class table and attendance.
House situated on high ground, commanding fine view of the Hudson River and the
great Poughkeepsie Bridge. References furnished on application.

MRS. WALTER CORLIES — Boarding house, Montgomery Street. One mile.
Accommodates 25. Rates $6 to $15 per week. First-class table and attendance.

HOPEWELL STATION — Hopewell Post Office.

DUANE ODELL — Farm house. Post office, Crouse's store. Five miles.
Accommodates 25. Adults, $6; children, half price; transients, $1 per day. Large
and convenient house, 100 foot piazza, shady grounds furnished with hammocks and
swings.

SALT POINT STATION — Salt Point Post office.

MRS. E. W. CONKLIN — Farm house. One and one-fourth miles. Accommodates 12. Adults, $6 to $7; children, at a reduction; transients, $1 per day. Free
transportation from station. Healthy location, shady grounds. Milk, eggs, vegetables, etc., from the farm. Large rooms, pleasant drives, daily mails. References
upon application.

MRS. H. A. LANSING — Farm house. One and one-half miles from Hibernia
station. Accommodates 10. $5 to $6 per week; reduction for children; transients,
$1 per day. Discount for season guests. Free transportation from station. Large,
shady lawn, pleasantly situated near stream of water. Fine drives and walks. Daily
mails, express and telegraph office. Good table and home comforts. References on
application.

HIBERNIA, DUTCHESS CO., N. Y.

A charming little hamlet, girt round about with swelling
hills and rich in facilities for out-door enjoyment. Numerous
small streams in the vicinity afford good fishing, while better
sport may be had at Lake Tyrell, a favorite tourists' resort,
three and a half miles south of the station.

Four miles from Hibernia is the handsome little town of
Millbrook, situated at a high altitude, in the midst of a
charming country noted for superb mountain scenery, ex-
ceptionably fine roads, beautiful walks and drives. As a
summer resort its popularity is rapidly growing. Millbrook
Inn, the principal hotel, is new, artistic, and perfectly appointed. Several other hotels and boarding houses furnish
first-class accommodations.

MRS. WILLIAM H. DOTY — Brookside farm house. Three-fourths mile. Accommodates 15. $5.50 to $6 per week ; $4 for children under 10 years of age; transients, $1 per day. Discount for season guests. Raises own vegetables. Fishing and boating on lake. Five minutes' walk to churches. Free transportation from station.

BENJAMIN H. TYRREL — Washington Hollow post office. Glenwood House. Accommodates 60. $7 to $10 per week ; children, half rates; transients, $2 per day. High ground ; splendid roads ; magnificent scenery ; fine, healthy climate ; good table ; pure water ; charming drives. Abundance of fruit and fresh vegetables. Lake 10 minutes' walk ; bass, pickerel and perch fishing. House open June 15th. Post office address until that date, 117 Bergen Street, Brooklyn. Refers to Judge Fitzsimmons, City Hall, New York ; Harry White, 316 President Street, Brooklyn ; George H. Doty, M. D., 129 Schermerhorn Street, Brooklyn.

H. H. VALENTINE — Halcyon Hall, Millbrook, N. Y. Four miles. Accommodates 250. Terms and particulars upon application. This is a modern, first-class house, erected last season. Beautifully situated, commanding fine views Elegant water. Send for illustrated pamphlet.

MILLBROOK INN. Four miles. Accommodates 150. Artistically and perfectly appointed. Write for particulars.

THOMAS WEATHERAL — Millbrook. Four miles. Accommodates 75. Adults, $25; children, $17.50; transients, $4 per day. Pure air, good roads. Gunning, etc. Will meet passengers if advised.

STANFORDVILLE, DUTCHESS CO., N. Y.

In this delightful region are many pleasant retreats which present superior attractions to the "summer boarder." Stanfordville itself is a charming village with a most picturesque environment. The massive bulk of Stissing Mountain, four miles to the northward, dominates the view in that direction, while in more immediate proximity the fertile valley farms smile back at generous Nature. Wappinger's Creek flows through the village, and Cold Spring Creek is near by. These streams afford excellent sport for the angler, while both fishing and boating may be indulged in upon Hunn's Lake, four miles east, and Upton's Lake, three miles southeast of the station. The places of worship are the Christian, Baptist, Methodist, and Roman Catholic Churches, and Friends' Meeting. There are good livery facilities convenient to the station.

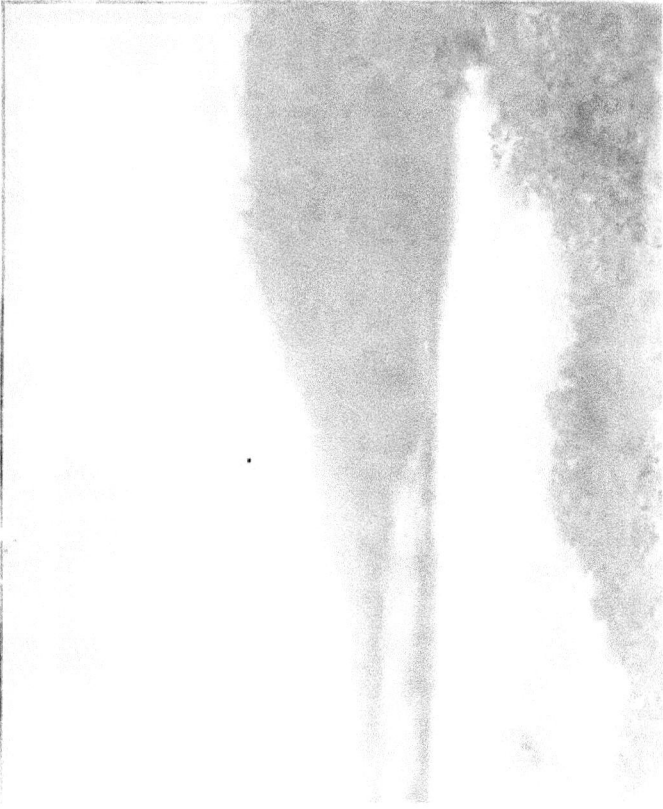

REUBEN A. HUSTED — Farm house. Five minutes' walk. Accommodates 20. Adults, $5; children at reduction; transients, $1 per day. Large and shady lawn. Small pond on place furnished with boats free to guests. Abundance of milk, eggs, and vegetables. Convenient to station, telegraph, and post office. Daily mails from New York. Refers to Mrs. William Allen, 13 Park Avenue, Brooklyn; Mr. Albert Lane, 337 Washington Avenue, Brooklyn.

ALBERT KNAPP — Farm house. One mile. Accommodates 10. Adults, $6; children, $4; transients, $1 per day. Large, airy rooms, good water, pleasant surroundings. Fishing and boating in lake. Discount for season guests. Will meet guests at station; no charge.

ALBERT J. HUSTED — Farm house. Two and one-half miles. Accommodates 12. Adults, $5 to $6; children, $4; transients, $1 per day. Free transportation from station. Table liberally supplied with farm products.

FRANK KNICKERBOCKER — Hotel. One-eighth mile. Accommodates 6. Adults, $7; transients, $1.25 per day. Located in a pleasant village. Fine drives. Stream of pure water near house. Trout, bass, and pickerel fishing.

O. P. WALTERMIRE — Farm house. Four miles. Accommodates 12. Adults $5 to $6; children at reduction; transients, $1 per day. Pleasantly situated on elevation of 2,000 feet; cool and breezy; shady lawns; excellent water; splendid scenery. Fishing and boating in lakes and streams near by. Vegetables from our own garden. Refers to J. F. Kelly, 264 Berry Street, Brooklyn; D. E. Anthony, 169 World Building, New York.

WM. M. WRIGHT — Bull's Head post office. Farm house. Two and one-half miles. Accommodates 20. Adults, $5 to $6; children at reduction; transients, $1 per day. House is beautifully located on an elevation of about 1,600 feet. No malaria nor mosquitoes. Large lawn and veranda. Abundance of fruit, vegetables, and farm produce. Bass and pickerel fishing. Refers to W. G. Turner, with E. S. Jaffray & Co., and John Borgwald, 223 N. 6th Avenue, Mount Vernon, N. Y.

ARTHUR D. BURNHAMS — Bull's Head post office. Farm house. Three miles. Accommodates 11. Adults, $6; children at reduction; transients, $1 per day. Has an elevation of 1,600 feet. Free transportation from station. Perfectly healthy, dry, pure air. No malaria nor mosquitoes. Large veranda. Fishing, etc. Refers to P. Grooth, N. Y. Life Insurance Co., 346 Broadway, New York, and H. Norman, 214 Prospect Avenue, Brooklyn.

GEORGE HYDE — Bangall post office. Farm house. One-half mile. Accommodates 20. Adults, $4; children, $2. Free transportation from station. Trout, bass, and pickerel fishing. Good livery accommodations. Raises own vegetables. Write for further particulars.

MRS. JOHN McLAUGHLIN — Bangall post office. Farm house. One mile. Accommodates 12. Adults, $5; children, $3. Large, shady grounds; good spring water. Fresh milk and butter. Pleasant rooms. Raises own vegetables. A pleasant summer home.

PERRY GREEN — Bangall post office. Farm house. Two miles. Accommodates 8. Rates, $6 to $7 per week; free transportation from station. Plenty of shade, fruit, eggs, and vegetables from our farm. House is pleasantly located; large, airy rooms; quiet neighborhood. Fishing in lakes and streams near by.

R. TALLMADGE — Hull's Mills post office. Farm house. Three and one-half miles. Accommodates 12. Rates, $6. Free transportation from station. House is situated on high ground. Fresh milk, eggs, and farm products. Excellent water. Pleasant lake short distance from the house, well equipped with boats. Fine drives and walks.

McINTYRE, DUTCHESS CO., N. Y.

The quietly pastoral character of the country hereabouts, with its wholesome air and generally healthful influences and its abounding picturesqueness, render it very desirable for a place of summer rest.

PINE PLAINS, DUTCHESS CO., N. Y.

This delightful village is located at the northern end of the Stissing Valley, in the afternoon shadow of Stissing Mountain, whose rounded peak towers a thousand feet above the plain. Along the eastern base of the mountain extends a chain of lakelets, two miles long, furnishing excellent fishing and boating, as well as many fine picnic resorts and rambles. These connected bodies of water are the head of Wappinger Creek, which winds in and out among the hills to join the Hudson. On the eastern and northern borders of the village a stream, called the Shacameco, flows through a beautiful valley, green-walled by lofty hills. The views from Pine Plains, and the elevated spots in its vicinity, are exceedingly grand, embracing the long range of the Ancram Hills, and extending twenty miles away to the Taconies, whose blue domes and wave-like crests form the background of a landscape of hill and valley, mountain and stream, forest and field, unsurpassed in variety and beauty.

The site of Pine Plains is glacial drift or deposit of gravel, securing natural drainage and ensuring perfect healthfulness. It is the boast of the inhabitants that there are in the village only two physicians, whose rides cover a radius of fifteen miles, and who yet have ample leisure to complain of "dull trade." There are Presbyterian, Methodist, Baptist, and Episcopalian churches, and a public school.

WM. H. TANNER — Farm house. One-quarter mile. Accommodates 10. Adults, $6; children, $3; transients, $1 per day. House is situated on the bank of Stissing Lake, a beautiful sheet of water surrounded with magnificent scenery. Pleasant drives and walks. Table liberally supplied with farm products. Free transportation from station in our own carriage. Further particulars on application.

M. L. WILLSON — Farm house. One and one-quarter miles. Accommodates 10. Adults, $6; children, half-price; transients, $1 per day. Free transportation from station. This house has kept summer boarders for many years and bears an excellent reputation. Fine scenery, walks, and drives. Fruit and vegetables in abundance. Further particulars on application.

RHINECLIFF, DUTCHESS CO., N. Y.

Starting again at the River Hudson, let us pass over the Rhinebeck Branch, which extends a distance of twenty-two miles from Rhinecliff to a connection with the main line at Silvernails.

Rhinecliff is on the east bank of the Hudson, sixteen miles north of the Great Bridge, and opposite the consolidated city of Kingston and Rondout. By means of a steam ferry to the latter point connection is effected with the Ulster and Delaware Railroad to and from all Catskill Mountain points. At Rhinecliff, also, connection is made in a union station with the New York Central and Hudson River Railroad.

The palace iron steamers of the Hudson River day line also make close connections at this point to and from all stations on our line and its immediate connections. The most charming inland water trip on the American continent and a delightful ride in comfortable coaches through the many points of interest herein mentioned can be made in a period of less than twelve hours' duration by taking steamers, daily, except Sunday, leaving Brooklyn (by annex) at 8 a. m.; New York, Desbrosses Street, 8.40, or 22d Street, North River, at 9 a. m. Meals are served at all hours in the restaurant on the boats, also *table d'hote* dinner, at $1.00 each, between the hours of 11 a. m. and 3 p. m. Returning, the Steamboat Express furnishes equally as good service, close connection being made with southbound steamer due at 22d Street, New York, at 5.30 p. m., Desbrosses Street 6 p. m., and Brooklyn 6.20 p. m.

"ALBANY."

OF THE DAY LINE, CONNECTING WITH STEAMBOAT EXPRESS AT RHINECLIFF, DAILY, EXCEPT SUNDAY.

RHINEBECK, DUTCHESS CO., N. Y.

This beautiful village is a favorite summer resort, with a number of excellent hotels and boarding-houses, three miles from the Hudson River. There is fishing on Lake Seepasco, in the vicinity, and the game consists of partridges, quail, woodcock, gray and red squirrel. There is a Lutheran church within a half mile, and five other places of worship within practicable distance.

RHINEBECK STATION — Rhinebeck Post Office.

JOHN M. WELCH — Farm house. One-half mile. Accommodates 20. Adults, $6 to $8; children, half price; transients, $1 per day. Table liberally supplied with fruits and vegetables from the farm. Boating and fishing in lakes near by. Gunning for small game. Send for circular. Refers to R. J. Dilworth, 420 Broadway, New York.

RED HOOK, DUTCHESS CO., N. Y.

A land of plenty this, where health and good living reign, six miles from the Hudson River. The air is light, clear, and invigorating, and local enthusiasts are wont to declare that their village possesses "the best drinking water in the State." The village contains three thriving churches— the Episcopalian, Methodist, and Lutheran. There is beautiful scenery in every direction, the mountain views being especially fine.

RED HOOK STATION — Red Hook Post Office.

A. J. GEDNEY — Boarding house. One-quarter mile. Accommodates 16. Adults, $6 to 8; transients, $1.25 per day. House is situated in a healthy locality, commanding splendid views. Excellent fishing; raises own vegetables. Free transportation if advised. Convenient to churches. Refers to the station agent.

THEODORE F. COOKINGHAM — Farm house. Four miles. Accommodates 12. Adults, $7; children, $4; transients $1.50 per day. Stage will meet guests if advised. Bass, pickerel, and trout fishing. Good livery accommodations. Refers to William Sittingham, 123 Fifth Avenue, New York.

JOHN A. FRALEIGH — Rose Hill Farm. One and one-half miles. Accommodates 12. Adults, $7; children, $3; transients, $1 per day. Will meet guests at station; no charge. Boating and fishing in numerous lakes and streams in vicinity. Pleasantly located on an elevation. Perfectly healthy, plenty of shade, extended views in all directions. Good roads, excellent water. Hot and cold water throughout the house. Refers to Mayor Schirien of Brooklyn, and Horatio Fowks, 11 Park Row, New York.

JAMES LEARY — Farm house. One and one-half miles. Accommodates 17. Adults, $5; children, $3; transients, $1 per day. Free conveyance from station. Table liberally supplied with vegetables, plenty of fresh milk, butter and eggs. Location healthy, fine mountain views, enough shade, fine walks and drives.

H. E. ELLSWORTH — Red Hook Hotel. One-fourth of a mile. Accommodates 50. Rates, $6 to $8 per week. Pleasantly located, first-class table, every convenience. Write for particulars.

R. G. MORE — Farm house. One mile. Rates, $6 to $8. Full particulars upon application.

MISS SARAH M. BOLINBAKER — Farm house. Two miles. Rates: Adults, $5; children half price. Accommodates 12. Free transportation from station.

FRANK NELSON — Farm house. Two miles. Accommodates 5. Adults, $5 to $7 per week. Full particulars upon application.

ELLERSLIE, COLUMBIA CO., N. Y.

Beautifully situated in a rich farming locality; good water; game in abundance. This is the nearest station to Eliza-ville, N. Y., three-quarters of a mile distant.

ELLERSLIE STATION — Elizaville Post Office.

Z. P. SMITH — Farm boarding house. One-half mile. Accommodates 20. Adults, $5 to $6; children, $3 to $4; transients, $1 per day. Free carriage from station. Raises own vegetables. Pickerel, perch, and bass fishing, boating, etc. Two beautiful lakes of over 70 acres each, within five minutes' walk of the house, with plenty of shade trees. Beautiful mountain scenery and natural waterfalls. A pleasant place to spend the summer. Refers to Charles O'Malley, 81 Fulton Street, New York.

J. N. COUSE — Farm house. One mile. Adults, $7. Full particulars upon application.

JACKSON CORNERS, DUTCHESS CO., N. Y.

This quiet little hamlet is located on the Rhinecliff Branch, eighteen miles from the Hudson River, and surrounded by a prosperous farming locality.

JACKSON CORNERS STATIONS — Jackson Corners Post Office.

PETER J. NEAR — Farm house. One and one-half miles. Accommodates 20. Rates upon application; transients, $1 per day. Free transportation from station, Mount Ross. Excellent fishing and boating in near by stream. House is situated on high, healthy grounds; has large, airy rooms. Raises own vegetables. Further particulars on application.

WILLIAM M. DECKER — Lafayetteville post office. Farm boarding house. Two and one-half miles. Accommodates 20. Adults, $5; children, $2.50; transients, $1 per day. Free transportation from station. Daily mails. Beautiful mountain scenery. References upon application.

29

MOUNT ROSS, DUTCHESS CO., N. Y.

Twenty miles back from the Hudson, and two miles from Silvernail Junction, with the main line in a farming locality.

SILVERNAILS STATION — Silvernails Post Office.

D. J. HEDGES — Farm house. Three-quarters of a mile. Accommodates 15. Adults, $7; children, $5; transients, $1.50 per day. Table liberally supplied with farm products. Small charge for meeting guests at station. House is beautifully located; plenty of shade; large, airy rooms. Fishing in streams and lakes near by.

ROBERT GRAY — Farm house, near station. Accommodates 8. Adults, $6; no children taken; discount for season guests. Raises own vegetables. Trout, bass, and pickerel fishing in lakes and streams near by. House is situated on the banks of the Ruloff Jansen Kill, noted for its grand scenery and natural falls. Plenty of shade. Home references on application.

J. A. HICKS — Farm house. One mile. Accommodates 7. Adults, $5 to $7; children, $3; transients, $1 per day. Free transportation from station. Excellent fishing and boating in Lake Charlotte, Jansen Kill, and Copake Lake. Pleasant neighborhood, excellent shade, romantic scenery, music, and various attractions. References on application.

JAMES FRITTS — Farm house. One-half mile. Accommodates 4. Adults, $5; children at reduction. House is situated on a hill commanding fine view of surrounding country. Raise our own vegetables. Excellent fishing and boating.

ANCRAM, COLUMBIA CO., N. Y.

This quiet village in Columbia County is emphatically a place of rest—a good place for tired people to go for a reposeful vacation. There are two churches—Lutheran and Methodist. The driving roads in the vicinity are excellent, the scenery varied and interesting, and there is exceptionally fine fishing, a number of small lakes within a short distance teeming with bass. The gunning is also very good, there being quail, woodcock, and partridge in abundance.

ANCRAM STATION — Ancram Post Office.

D. KISSELBACK — Hotel. One-fourth mile. Accommodates 20. Adults, $7; children, $5; transients, $2 per day. This house has reputation of setting first-class table. Eight lakes and ponds within easy distance; fine drives, beautiful scenery, varied and interesting. Good livery accommodations.

MRS. GEORGE WOODARD — Private residence. One-fourth mile. Accommodates 10. Adults, $4 to $6; children, half price; transients, $1 per day. Free transportation from station. A perfectly healthy location. Pure spring water. Shade. No mosquitoes. Fresh milk, eggs, and vegetables; fruit in season; excellent fishing. Convenient to churches. A good place to spend the summer. Refers to Mrs. Arthur Whitehead, 272 14th Street, South Brooklyn; George Miller, 528 5th Avenue, South Brooklyn.

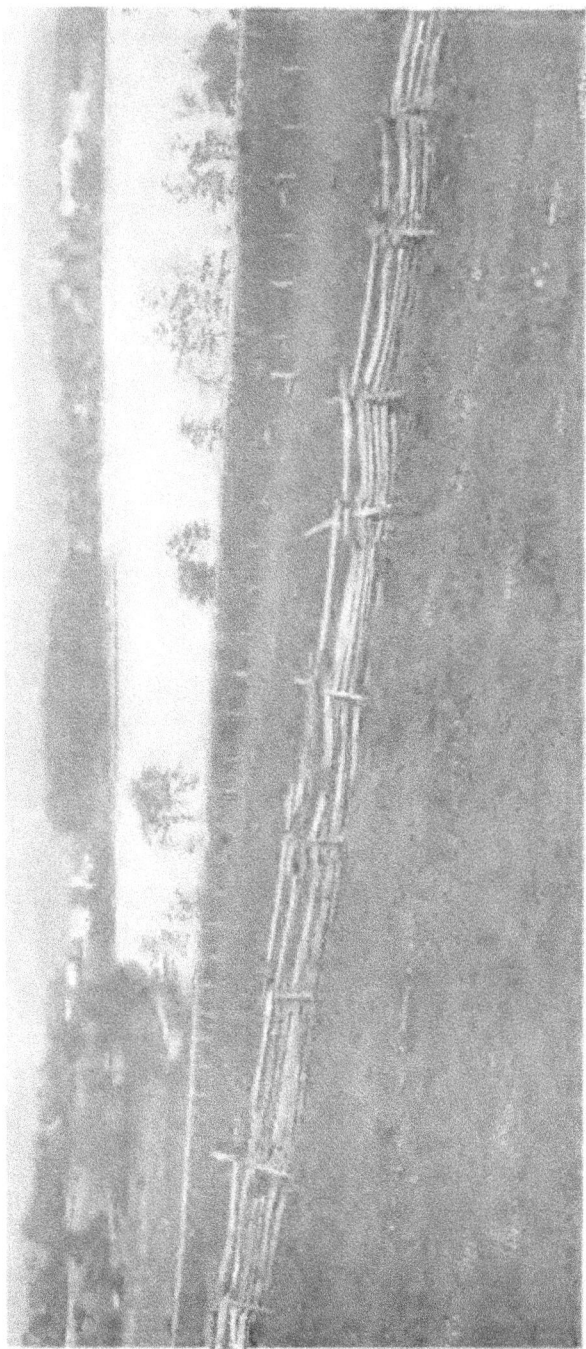

"LAKE WONONSCOPONUC", LAKEVILLE.

HENRY W. DOWNING — Farm house. Two miles. Accommodates 6. Rates
$6 to $8; children, $3; transients, $1 per day. Free transportation from station.
House is situated near the banks of a nice stream; good bathing facilities, excellent
roads and pleasant walks. Picturesque mountain scenery. Raises own vegetables.
Lake and river fishing. Refers to the Hon. Wallace Bruce, ex-consul to Edinburgh,
Brooklyn, N. Y., and F. A. D. Chase, Esq., Hudson, N. Y.

A. KILMER — Hotel. One-fourth mile. Accommodates 10. Weekly rates on
application; transients, $1 per day. Raises own vegetables. Good fishing and near
by lakes and streams. Livery accommodations, etc.

COPAKE, COLUMBIA CO., N. Y.—MT. WASHINGTON, MASS.

Copake forms the gateway to Mount Washington, and
the two may properly be considered together. Here the
landscape presents bolder outlines, and we realize that we
are approaching the highlands. In the vicinity of Copake
there is excellent trout fishing, also pleasant drives and delightful scenery in every direction.

Mount Washington is a township in the southwestern
corner of Berkshire County, Massachusetts. It comprises a
lofty plateau, several miles in extent, with an elevation of
two thousand feet, and is surrounded with mountain peaks
which tower several hundred feet higher, the highest being
Mount Everett, which rises to an altitude of twenty-seven
hundred feet. This town among the clouds is one of the
richest spots in picturesque scenery in Eastern America,
and the whole impressive landscape when bathed in sunshine looks as if

"Touched by a light that hath no name,
A glory never sung;
Aloft on sky and mountain wall
Are God's great pictures hung."

It is rapidly becoming known and renowned for its delightful summer temperature, dryness and purity of the
atmosphere, and increased electric tension due to an abundance of ozone and sunshine. It is not only a most desirable retreat for invalids, but a favorite summer resort for
pleasure seekers as well.

MRS. J. E BELLOWS, NORFOLK.

EAST WINSTED PARK.

STEVENS HOUSE, NORFOLK.

NEWGATE PRISON, TARIFFVILLE. 200 YEARS OLD.

It is reached by a seven miles' drive from Copake, over a level road as far as Copake Iron Works; thence by a sharp ascent of an excellent road along the north bank of the famed Bash-Bish, which comes down through a cleft in the mountains for two miles. This portion of the drive, all the way skirting the rushing waters of the stream and passing the famous Bash-Bish Falls, is indescribably grand and beautiful. Emerging from the gorge we enter the broad, uplifted valley which constitutes the town of Mount Washington.

COPAKE STATION — Copake Post Office.

M. HOLSAPPLE — Hotel. One-half mile. Accommodates 25. Rates, $5 to $8 per week. Full particulars on application.

W. VAN DE BOGART — Hotel. One-half mile. Accommodates 25. Rates, $5 to $8 per week. Particulars on application.

S. J. BARNET — Copake Iron Works P. O. Hotel. Three miles. Rates, $5 to $8 per week. Particulars on application.

L. COOK — Copake Iron Works P. O. Hotel. Three miles. Rates, $5 to $8 per week. Particulars on application.

WILLIAM H. WEAVER — Boarding-house. Mount Washington, Mass. Five miles. Accommodates 35. Rates, $5 to $9 per week. Particulars on application.

IRA L. PATTERSON -- Boarding-house. Mount Washington, Mass. Accommodates 25. Rates, $5 to $9 per week.

I. SPURR — Boarding-house. Mount Washington, Mass. Accommodates 40. Rates, $5 to $9 per week.

FRANK SHUTT — Boarding-house. Mount Washington, Mass. Accommodates 15. Terms, $5 to $9 per week.

O. C. WHITBECK — Boarding-house, Mount Washington, Mass. Accommodates 35. Rates $5 to $9 per week.

F. H. KEITH — Boarding-house, Mount Washington, Mass. Accommodates 12.

BOSTON CORNERS, COLUMBIA CO., N. Y.

This is a pleasant little town, possessing a certain curious interest, which will long be remembered as the place where the famous prize fight between Morrissey and Yankee Sullivan occurred. At the point where the " ring was pitched " one can step from the State of New York into Connecticut or Massachusetts. There is good fishing hereabouts, trout and pickerel being plentiful. The mountain scenery is extremely fine, and the roads in the vicinity are excellent.

BOSTON CORNERS STATION — Boston Corners Post Office.

C. J. SMITH — Mount Airy Cottage. One-fourth mile. Accommodates 12. Adults, $6 to $7; children on application; transients, $1.25 per day. House stands on high ground overlooking the village; scenery unsurpassed. Bracing mountain air. No mosquitoes nor malaria. Fishing and boating in lakes near by.

MRS. A. M. RECORD — Hotel, near station. Accommodates 15. Adults, $7; children, $4; transients, $1.50 per day. Hotel is located on a small bluff at foot of Taghanic Mountains. Piazza on two sides, from which many beautiful and interesting views may be had. Excellent fishing and boating. Good livery accommodations.

MOUNT RIGA, DUTCHESS CO., N. Y.

The village has a population of about five hundred. It lies in a valley three-fourths of a mile wide, bounded on the east by the mountain from which it derives its name, and on the west by a range of high hills running north about four miles. The principal or most prominent hill, called "Cave Hill," is directly opposite the village, and is covered by a handsome forest growth. On a steep side of this hill is an extensive cave, which, to a depth of four hundred feet, contains apartments fifty feet high. It has never been fully explored farther than four hundred feet from its mouth, owing to the narrowness of the passage at that point.

MOUNT RIGA STATION — Mount Riga Post Office.

R. P. SMITH — Chestnut Hill Cottage. One and one-quarter miles. Accommodates 15. Adults, $6 to $8; children, $4; transients, $1.25 per day. Free transportation from station. House stands on a hillside overlooking the Harlem valley; elevation 1,400 feet. Pure, bracing mountain air. Convenient to the famous Bash-Bish Falls, Mount Washington, Twin Lakes, and other points of interest. Excellent lake fishing and boating. Table supplied with fresh and pure farm products. References on application.

MILLERTON, DUTCHESS CO., N. Y.

There are few places that can offer greater attractions and advantages for a summer sojourn than Millerton. It is situated on high ground with charming surroundings, is exceedingly healthy, and enjoys cool nights in the warmest weather.

At this point connection is made with the fast express trains on the Harlem Division of the New York Central & Hudson River road to and from Grand Central Station, New York, through car service between New York and Winsted being maintained on train leaving New York, daily, except Sunday, at 3.40 P. M., returning on train due at New York at 11.50 A. M. It is also expected that connection will be made with the Saturday half-holiday and Monday morning specials during the coming season.

MILLERTON STATION — Millerton Post Office.

J. L. BARTON — Hotel. Accommodates 60. $7 per week. Particulars on application.

MRS. W. B. GREY — Park Street boarding-house. Accommodates 8. Adults, $7 per week.

ROBERT KAYE — Millerton House. Accommodates 25. Adults, $8; children, $5.

ORRIN WAKEMAN — Maple Shade Farm. Accommodates 10. Adults, $6 to $7; children, $4 to $5.

FRANK SILVERNAIL. — Central Hotel. Accommodates 75. Terms, $7 and upwards for adults and $5 for children.

ORE HILL, LITCHFIELD CO., CONN.

This pretty village has numerous attractions to offer to those in search of summer homes.

ORE HILL STATION—Ore Hill Post Office.

MRS. EMMA EVERTS — Farm house. One-half mile. Accommodates 6. Adults, $7; children, $5; transients, $1 per day. Beautiful scenery. Excellent fishing and boating in lakes near by. Livery accommodations. Table supplied with farm products.

LAKEVILLE.

LAKEVILLE, LITCHFIELD CO., CONN.

A pleasant village, whose name is derived from its most prominent natural feature—a beautiful lake, the Indian name of which, Wononscopomuc, signifies "clear water." Two good-sized lakes afford boating, bathing, and fishing. The scenery revealed by the many fine drives in the vicinity is diversified and picturesque. The Hotchkiss Yale Preparatory School is located here, and there are churches of several denominations. The town was settled by the English in 1720, and is replete with traditions and scenes of historic and picturesque interest. The visitor is shown a well, near the station, from which Ethan Allen once quaffed a crystal bumper. The surrounding country is intersected with good roads, giving access to numerous pleasant and beautiful places.

The Hotchkiss School was opened October 19, 1892. It owes its foundation to Mrs. Maria H. Hotchkiss, a native of Salisbury, who has already expended about $200,000 on the buildings and surrounding land, besides endowing the school with an educational fund of $200,000 more.

The work of the school is the preparation of boys for college. Though enjoying in an extraordinary degree the good will of Yale University, its course of instruction makes impartial and amplest recognition of the requirements of both Yale and Harvard colleges, and its roll includes students preparing for both institutions.

The school has already won a national reputation. Students are in attendance not only from every section of the country, but also from foreign countries, and it has been impossible to keep up with the applications for admission. During the first year the accommodations were limited to fifty boys; this year sixty-seven are provided for. The total attendance, including day scholars, is seventy-two. It is intended that the attendance shall never exceed two hundred.

Bissell Hall, now building, will be available in September, and will provide accommodations for forty more boys.

Requests for catalogues should be sent to EDWARD G. COY, Head Master.

Enquire of G. B. Burrall, Lakeville.

LAKEVILLE STATION—Lakeville Post Office.

D. LAWRENCE SHAW—Hotel, boarding-house, and four cottages. One mile. Accommodates 100. Special rates upon application. Carriage from station. Special arrangement for season guests. Excellent sailing, boating, and fishing. Pure mountain air; no mosquitoes nor malaria. One of the most delightful spots to be found in this country. See description of Lakeville.

EUGENE L. PEABODY—Wononsco House. One-eighth mile. Accommodates 60. Adults, $8 and upward; children, $5; transients, $2 per day. Beautiful location. Finest drives in New England. Excellent boating, bathing, fishing, and hunting; in fact, everything for a pleasant, comfortable summer home.

MRS. SARAH E. BRADLEY — Farm house. One mile. Accommodates 10. Adults, $7; children, $5; transients, $1 per day. This is a large, two-story house, with good-sized airy rooms. The finest scenery; elegant, pure spring water. One-half mile from Hotchkiss Yale Preparatory School. Fishing, sailing, and every summer enjoyment.

WM. B. PERRY — Private boarding-house. Three minutes' walk. Accommodates 25. Adults, $10 and upward. Excellent fishing in numerous lakes and streams. Boating, bathing, and sailing. Every attraction for a pleasant summer home. Convenient to churches. Good livery accommodations.

MRS. E. BLODGETT — Summer boarding-house. One-fourth mile. Accommodates 15. Adults, $7 to $12; children, special only; transients, $2 per day. House is of colonial style, with large lawn and fine shade. Ample stable and carriage room. Boating, bathing, and fishing.

MRS. O. G. BRADLEY — Farm house. One mile. Accommodates 12. Adults, $5 and upward; children, special. Suitable arrangements made for season guests. Raises own vegetables. Every summer attraction at this place.

JOHN S. PERKINS — Farm house. One mile. Accommodates 12. Adults, $6 and upward; children and transients, special. Discount for season guests. Table liberally supplied with farm products. For further particulars see description of Lakeville.

MRS. E. J. DAKIN — Boarding-house. One-eighth mile. Accommodates 12. $6 and upward; children, $5 and upward. Table liberally supplied with fresh farm products. A pleasant summer home.

DARWIN D. WARNER — Farm house. One mile. Accommodates 12. Adults, $8; children at reduced rates; transients, $1.25 per day. Large grounds beautifully shaded by maples. Elegant piazza; bay windows. Beautiful scenery. Two of the finest lakes in the country near by. Pure and bracing mountain air. Excellent fishing in lakes. Good livery accommodations. An enjoyable spot to pass the sultry weather.

SALISBURY, LITCHFIELD CO., CONN.

This is a thriving village in the heart of the iron district of Connecticut. An object of interest here are the mines of iron ore, which have been worked since 1734. Here, also, is situated Sage's Ravine, through which for a mile or more a clear mountain stream, icy-cold even in midsummer, plunges through a dense forest by successive leaps from a few feet to a great fall of sixty or more. About one mile north of this a stream flowing from Plantain Pond, which nestles in the woods among the hills, one thousand feet above the Housatonic, after flowing a quarter of a mile through a wild forest, plunges over an almost perpendicular cliff, nearly five hundred feet, and disappears in the forest below.

MAIN STREET, SALISBURY.

From the top of the forest-covered cliff over which these waters plunge one of the finest views in New England is obtained. With the roaring brook at your back, rushing onward through the forest to its final plunge, you look down upon a scene which lingers long in the memory of all who witness it. Bear Mountain is also located near here. On this mountain rests a landmark declaring that this is the highest land in the State; it is a stone monument in the shape of a pyramid, thirty feet high, erected in 1885 and rebuilt in 1888.

About here is a wilderness of the most extravagant, rugged mountain scenery, savage and irregular in its wild but fascinating features, and where a tired soul will find a locality the surroundings of which will afford him the relief he seeks in infinite repose.

In Salisbury there are two places of worship, Episcopalian and Congregational, and three grades of schools. The fishing and hunting in the neighborhood are excellent.

SALISBURY STATION—Salisbury Post Office.

MRS. M. RUSSELL.—Boarding-house. One eighth mile. Accommodates 45. Rates, $8 to $10 for adults; children, $5 to $7; transients, $2 per day. House is situated on east side of Main Street, surrounded by maple shade. Spacious grounds, commanding a fine view of the mountains. Fine drives and walks in every direction. Excellent spring water. Table liberally supplied with fresh vegetables from the farm. Bass, pickerel, and trout fishing in lakes and streams near by. New York and Brooklyn references upon application.

MRS. J. M. ODENBREIT—Sunnyside Farm. Accommodates 14. $6 to $7 for adults; children, half price. High elevation; pleasant, shady grounds. No malaria nor mosquitoes. Splendid scenery. Excellent fishing. Will meet guests at station. Location, one and one-half miles from Twin Lakes.

MRS. J. G. LANDON—Lawn Cottage. One-third mile. Accommodates 30. Terms, $8 to $10 per week; special rates for families. Beautifully situated. Large, airy rooms. Pleasant walks and drives; finest in the state. Excellent fishing and boating in lakes near by. Write for further particulars.

TWIN LAKES.

CHAPINVILLE, LITCHFIELD CO., CONN.

The surrounding country is rich in farms, iron mines, delightful drives, lakes well stocked with fish, and historical reminiscences, while its healthfulness is established beyond question by such evidences as the absence of malarial influences, and the long and contented lives of its happy inhabitants.

CHAPINVILLE STATION—Chapinville Post Office.

WILLIAM J. CLARK—Farm house. One-eighth mile. Accommodates 15. Terms, $8 to $10: transients, $2 per day. House and rooms large and convenient. Elegant shade, lawn, and piazza : beautiful view of the lake. Finest drives in the world. Stabling for horses. Celebrated Sage's Ravine only one and one-half miles distant. Excellent trout and pickerel fishing. Raises own vegetables. Pure mountain air ; no mosquitoes nor malaria. Carriages free from station. References on application.

TWIN LAKES, LITCHFIELD CO., CONN.

This is a well known and favorite locality for camping and fishing parties. Trout, black bass, and pickerel, and many other varieties of fish, swarm in the lakes, and speckled trout are plentiful in the numerous streams. The place is easily reached from the neighboring towns and villages, and boats can be hired and guides obtained at extremely reasonable rates. It is a veritable sportsmen's paradise, yet it is just as prolific of delight to the lover of nature who may come here innocent of harmful design against the feathered, furred, and finned inhabitants of these woods and waters.

The scenery is wild, grand, and impressive in its loveliness and loneliness. The sparkling wavelets laugh at the sombre forests that girdle them about, while far away the solemn mountain shapes rise in purple majesty.

" White clouds whose shadows haunt the deep !
Light mists whose soft embraces keep
The sunshine on the hills asleep !

O, Isles of calm! O, dark still wood!
And stiller skies that overbrood
Your rest with deeper quietude!

O, shapes and hues, dim beckoning, through
Yon mountain-gaps, my longing view
Beyond the purple and the blue,

To stiller sea and greener land,
And softer lights and airs more bland,
And skies, the hollow of God's hand!"

CANAAN, LITCHFIELD CO., CONN.
THE BERKSHIRE HILLS.

Canaan is one of the chief gateways to that land of beauty, the Berkshire Hills. It is also an excellently convenient rendezvous and headquarters for tourists and vacationists visiting Twin Lakes and other resorts in this region. The village is a pleasant place in all respects; there are five churches, good schools, and agreeable society. The vicinity furnishes first-rate fishing and hunting.

Of the Berkshire Hills someone has written: "It is a region of hill and valley, mountain and lake, beautiful rivers, and laughing brooks." But to convey to those who have never reveled among the manifold delights of this New England Arcadia, an adequate idea of its attractions is probably beyond the scope of human ability. The magnificence of its diversified scenery, the wonderfully vitalizing effects of its pure atmosphere, the phenomenal healthfulness that characterizes life in its lofty villages and hamlets, have made the Berkshire region one of the most advantageous and altogether desirable of all of our summer resorts. These hills are a continuation of the Green Mountain Range, and cover an area of twenty miles in length by fifty in breadth. The highest peak is Greylock Mountain, which attains an altitude of thirty-five hundred feet.

There are numerous pleasant villages from which to select a summer abode, the most prominent being Great Barrington, Stockbridge, Lee, Lenox, Pittsfield, and North Adams, all in the State of Massachusetts.

To reach any one of these places from points west of the Hudson River, and also from some points east of Canaan, the "Poughkeepsie Bridge Line" is by far the preferable route.

CANAAN, CONN.—Canaan Post Office.

E. W. WARNER — "Warner House." Near station. Accommodates 50. Terms, $6 to $10. House is beautifully situated in the village and makes a very comfortable summer home. Particulars on application.

EAST CANAAN STATION—East Canaan Post Office.

NATHANIEL BEEBE — Boarding-house. Near station. Accommodates 6. Adults, $7. House is located in a rich farming section, surrounded by hills. Write for particulars.

MRS. L. F. BRONSON — Farm house. One-fourth mile. Accommodates $8. Adults, $6; children, at reduction; transients, $1 per day. Free transportation from station. Table liberally supplied with farm products, poultry, and milk from our Jersey cows. Trout fishing in streams near by. Half mile from church and post office. References furnished on application.

MRS. ALICE ANDRUS — Private house. Near station. Accommodates 6. Adults, $7 per week. Full particulars on application.

TWIN LAKES STATION—Chapinville Post Office.

THOMAS O'HARA — Farm boarding-house. Two miles. Accommodates 20. Terms, $7 to $9; children, $3 to $5; transients, $1.50 per day. House is beautifully situated, grand scenery. Elevation about 1,000 feet. Free from malaria and mosquitoes. Excellent spring water. Fine drives. House is about 200 feet from the shore of the lake. Excellent bass, pickerel, and trout fishing, boating and bathing. Table liberally supplied with farm products. Building lots on the shore of the lake for sale at reasonable prices. References on application.

MRS. W. R. WHEELER — Summer cottage. One and one-fourth miles. Accommodates 6. Rates $1 per day. House is beautifully located near the lake. Raises own vegetables. Guests will be met at station if desired; charge, 50 cents. Mrs. Wheeler's address before June 15th will be 60 Tremont Street, Hartford, Conn. Write for particulars.

CHARLES J. SMITH — Summer cottage. One-half mile. Accommodates 15. Rates, $1 per day. House situated in Twin Lakes grove on shore of the lake. Pure spring water. Fresh vegetables from our own truck patch. Fishing, boating, sailing. Fishing outfits, boats, and bait furnished at small charge. Large dancing pavilion. Every attention paid to comforts of our visitors.

GREAT BARRINGTON, MASS.— Great Barrington Post Office, via Canaan.

MISS CELESTE HULBERT — Cottage. Five minutes' walk. Accommodates 7. Terms upon application. House is entirely new, opposite a beautiful grove. Spring water. Will rent furnished or unfurnished. Inquire of owner on premises or by mail. References furnished.

SUMMER HOME OF CLARA LOUISE KELLOGG, NEW HARTFORD.

SOLDIERS' MONUMENT, WINSTED.

RESIDENCE OF MR. WITTER, LAKEVILLE.

RESIDENCE OF GOV. HOLLEY, LAKEVILLE.

NORFOLK, LITCHFIELD CO., CONN., LITCHFIELD HILLS.

Norfolk, in the heart of the Litchfield Hills, adjacent to Berkshire County, is the highest town in the State reached by railroad, lying thirteen hundred feet above the sea. The air is pure and bracing, and entirely free from malaria. The town has become one of the most favorite summer resorts in the State, and is filled with several hundred boarders during the summer and autumn.

The scenery and numerous picturesque drives add greatly to the attractive features of Norfolk. From the belvidere on the summit of Haystack Mountain can be seen large stretches of land in New York, Massachusetts, and Connecticut; also the Bear Mountain Monument, marking the highest ground in Connecticut (twenty-three hundred and fifty-four feet), Ivy Mountain Tower, the monument on Monument Mountain in New York, Talcott Mountain Tower near Hartford, the beautiful mountains of the Taghanic range, and numbers of the Berkshire Hills.

It is needless to say that so popular a center of tourist and summer travel is well supplied with facilities for the accommodation of strangers.

> "The tempest may dash on the vale and hill,
> But the sunshine smiles behind it;
> The caverned rock hides the mountain rill,
> Yet a tiny gleam can find it.
> Gladness will fall upon grief's cold breast
> And soften the voice of its warning,
> Over the darkness sweet hope will rest,
> And after the shadows—comes morning."

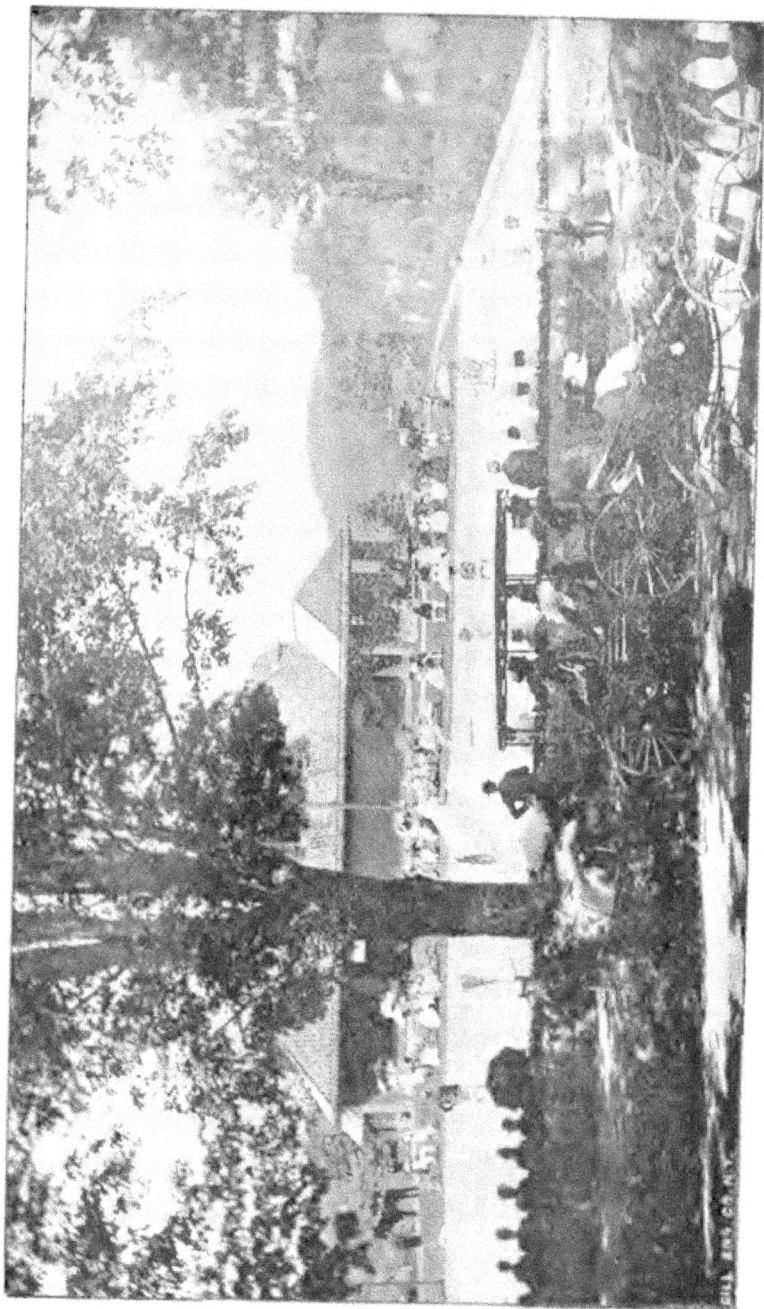

NORFOLK.

A. E. McLEAN—"Hillhurst." One-fourth mile. Accommodates 100. Adults, $15 to $25 per week ; transients, $3 to $3.50 per day. This house is situated on a hill overlooking the beautiful and popular summer resort of Norfolk, and is within ten minutes' walk of churches, post office, railroad station, and green. The elevation of the house is 1,300 feet above sea level. Beautiful and extensive views, pure mountain air, cool and bracing. House contains 76 rooms, handsomely furnished. Open fire-places in reading-room. Three parlors, assembly and smoking-room set apart for use of guests. Dining-room seats 125 persons. Table first class in every respect. Piazza 150 feet long and 10 feet wide runs entire length of house. House is supplied with pure spring water from the mountains. Diagram of house will be sent on application.

C. E. STEVENS—"Stevens House." One-fourth mile. Accommodates 75. Rates, $10 to $20 per week for adults ; transients, $2 to $2.50 per day. This is a popular family house, well located in village, and gives special attention to summer boarders. Table is first class in every respect. Free transportation from station. Fishing and boating in lakes near by. Church and post office convenient. No malaria nor mosquitoes. Good livery accommodations at reasonable prices. City references furnished on application.

MRS. E. J. BELLOWS—Private house. One-eighth mile. Accommodates 18. Adults, $10 to $12 ; children, at reduction; transients, $2 per day. Table supplied with fine vegetables from our own garden. Good fishing in lakes near by. Small game. Excellent livery accommodations. Convenient to church and post office. Free transportation from station. Discount for season guests.

EDGAR L. COLE—Private house. One-half mile. Nine rooms. Will rent house furnished for the coming season, also barn. Situated on Laurel Way, about half mile from station and church. House contains bath-room and is pleasantly located. Write for particulars and terms.

C. K. NORTHWAY—South Norfolk post office. Four miles. Accommodates 8. Adults, $6; discount for season guests. Trout fishing. Pure mountain air and a very pleasant summer resting place. Write for particulars.

ERASTUS S. JOHNSON—Farm and house to rent. Farm contains 300 acres. Will sell, or rent with house and barn for summer. Two miles from railroad and one-eighth mile from Tamarack Lodge. House is situated on road which is traveled by summer boarders every day. Has parlor, sitting-room, dining-room, ten bed-rooms, two pantries. Mr. Johnson will be found at the Norfolk livery stable.

JAMES F. BEACH—Grantville post office. Nearest station, Grant's. Three-fourths mile. Accommodates 20. Adults, $10; children, $5 per week ; transients, $2 per day. Discount for season guests. Free transportation from station. House is situated on an elevation 1,400 feet above the sea, on the summit of the mountain; park adjoining house ; views of many mountains miles and miles away. Beautiful lake few yards distant. Fine drives, lovely flower gardens, etc. Excellent fishing and boating. First-class team on the premises. References furnished on application.

NEW MARLBORO INN (among the Berkshire Hills), New Marlboro, Mass. All the advantages of a hotel with the comforts of a home. Situated in the most charming spot among the famous Berkshire Hills — the Switzerland of America. Fourteen hundred and eighty feet above the sea level. Five hundred feet higher than any other resort in the county. Thus located, the Inn affords absolutely pure and invigorating atmosphere, entirely free from mosquitoes and malaria, and an opportunity unapproached by any other locality in Berkshire County, for the weary and overtaxed to recuperate, and the young to acquire strength. The advantages for pleasure and recreation are unbounded. The numerous mountain streams abound with beautiful brook trout, bass, and pickerel. Rooms commanding any exposure, and in any portion of the house, may be secured upon application. Our season opens June 15. Applications for board will receive prompt attention. Terms : $10 to $15 per week. Special rates made with families. A. F. Campbell & Co., Proprietors, New Marlboro, Berkshire County, Mass.

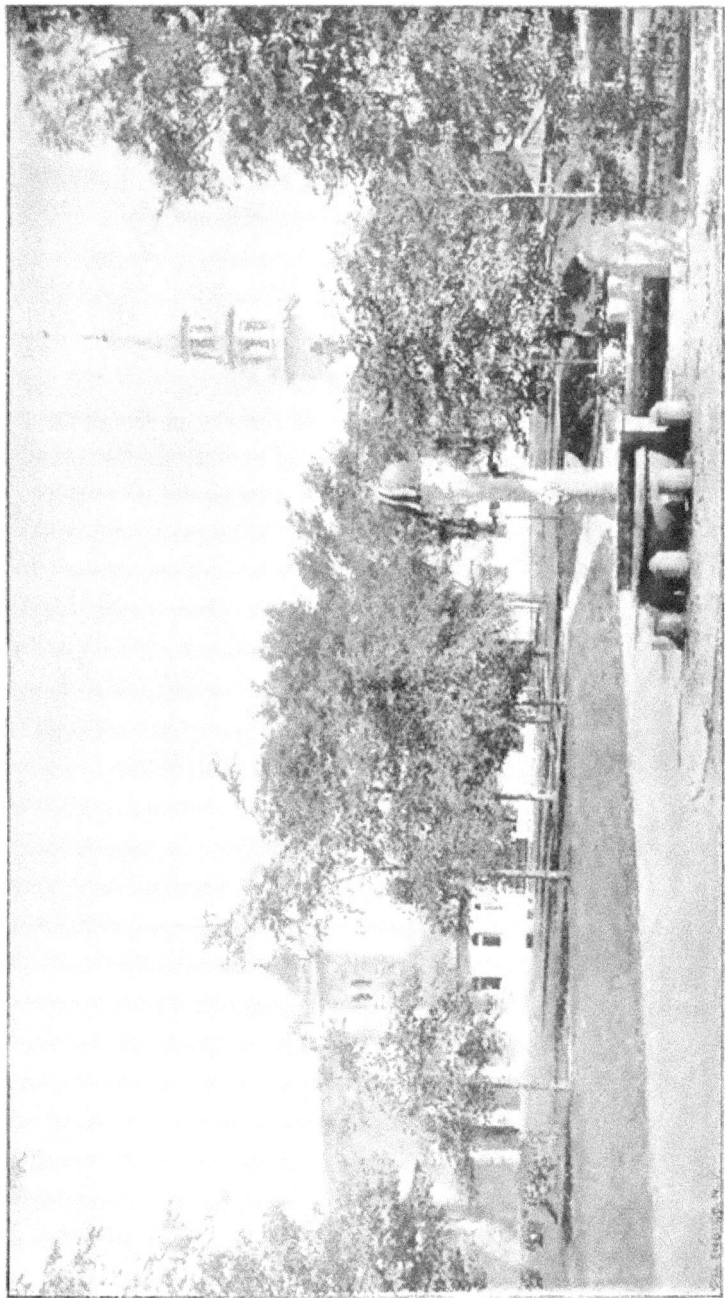

NORFOLK.

WEST WINSTED, LITCHFIELD CO., CONN.

Winsted is a charming town, nestling on the hills that form the banks of the Still and Mad Rivers. The scenery about Winsted is naturally picturesque, for it combines both the pleasant stretches of the valley and the rugged beauty of the highland. Tree-crowned heights are interspersed with barren peaks, that recall the cosmic convulsions of primeval days; and as the town extends the picture is varied and beautified by attractive homes. Highland Lake, on the west side of Winsted, nine hundred feet above tide water, is a fairy-like sheet—deep, dark, still, and clear —three miles long, abounding with bass, pickerel, and perch, with steep, rock-faced hills and woody capes, overhanging and casting their broad shadows across its surface.

The Philadelphia, Reading & New England Railroad has in this place three stations—West Winsted, Winsted, and East Winsted. Combined they form a city of about seven thousand inhabitants, with churches of all denominations and all the surroundings and conveniences of city life, while yet retaining all its country charms.

HIGHLAND LAKE, WINSTED.

WINSTED.

GEORGE H. SPENCER — Beardsley House. Two minutes' walk. Accommodates 100. Adults, $10 and upwards; children, $7 and up. Transients, $2 and $2.50 per day. Free bus from station, except for baggage. Passenger elevator, electric lights and bells, and gas. Billiard parlor, baths, etc. Sanitary arrangements perfect. Table is liberally supplied with the choicest provisions that can be secured. The open exposure of the rooms admit f abundance of sunlight and fresh air. The interior arrangements are designed to secure privacy of family and still obtain the comforts of a first class hotel service; all combine to make this house one of the most popular in the State. See cut of house below. Refers to William C. E. Bolles, 12 Village Street, Hartford; John T. Rockwell, 175 William Street, New York; W. H. Jenks, 375 6th Street, Brooklyn.

GEORGE W. LEE — Cottage. Two and one-half miles. Accommodates 10. Terms upon application. House is situated near Highland Lake, five minutes' walk from steamboat landing. Broad piazza. Fine grove near by. An excellent place to pass the heated term.

W. B. WILSON — Pavilion. Three miles. Reached by steamer on Highland Lake every hour; fare, 10 cents. Bass and pickerel fishing. Boats to let. The pavilion is beautifully located. Meals are served at all hours. Seven rooms for lodging. Fine grounds covering ten acres, with shrubbery and shade. A trip to this resort is always enjoyed.

BEARDSLEY HOUSE.

WINSTED STATION—Winsted Post Office.

C. B. ANDREWS — Hotel Andrews. One-eighth mile. Accommodates 100. Rates, $6 to $12; children, $6; transients, $2 to $2.50 per day. Long, wide piazza; large parlors, first-class dining-room, seating 125 people; large, airy sleeping-rooms. Shade trees and lawn, making this one of the coolest resorts in town. Location central, within five minutes' walk of seven churches. Bass, pickerel, and trout fishing.

BEARDSLEY HOUSE DINING-ROOM.

ARTHUR M. GRANT — Central house. One-eighth mile. Accommodates 35. Adults, $7; children under eight years old, $5; transients, $1.25 per day. House is situated in the town of Winsted, which is surrounded by many points of interest to summer boarders. Refers to all business firms in the city.

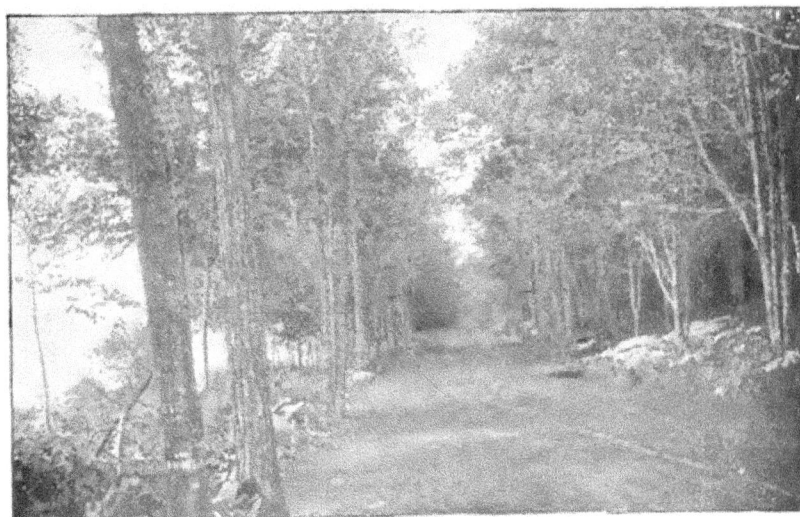

WINSTED.

NEW HARTFORD, LITCHFIELD CO., CONN.

The village of New Hartford lies in the basin of the Farmington River, at an elevation of nine hundred feet above the level of the sea. On all sides it is surrounded by picturesque hills and towering mountains. The scenery is uncommonly fine, some of the views, as will be seen by the illustrations, being exceedingly beautiful. The vicinity of the village abounds in pleasantly-shaded drives, and there is good fishing in the lakes and streams within convenient distance. Many city people summer here, and, while we are unable to furnish a list of boarding-houses, anyone coming to this hospitable little town will have no difficulty in securing agreeable quarters.

PINE MEADOW STATION—Pine Meadow Post Office.

WILLIAM CAUL — Boarding house. One mile. Accommodates 25. Adults, $7; children, $2 to $4; transients, $1.25 per day. Good spring water. Excellent fishing in the Farmington River. Raises own vegetables. Convenient cottages and lodging places to be had near by. Guests will be met at station with private carriage, 50 cents.

CANTON STATION—Canton Post Office.

HENCY C. WALES — Canton Hotel. One-eighth mile. Accommodates 12. Adults, $8; children, $6; transients, $2 per day. Free transportation from station. House stands at foot of the mountain. Excellent walks and drives in all directions. Fine, shady grove near house. Rooms large and airy, clean and good beds. Excellent table guaranteed. References on application.

SIMSBURY, HARTFORD CO., CONN.

This is a typical New England village, a quiet place, with broad, well-shaded streets and a pervading air of thrift, comfort, and repose. It is favored as a summer resting-place by those seeking a pleasant retreat within easy distance of the large centers of population.

SIMSBURY, CONN.

J. B. McLEAN—Boarding School Buildings. One-half mile. Accommodates 40 adults. $10 to $12; children, $6 to $8. Large, pleasant rooms. Beautifully located. First-class table. Write for further particulars.

SIMSBURY STATION—Weatogue Post Office.

MRS. C. J. MARKS— Private house. Five miles. Accommodates 7. Adults, $7 to $8; children, $5. Write for particulars.

NEW HARTFORD.

At Tariffville, the railroad and Farmington River pass side by side through Talcott Mountain. The scenery in this vicinity is quite picturesque. On the summit of the mountain, one-third of a mile distant from the Tower Station, stands the Bartlett Tower, the view from which is marvelous. Although only six hundred feet above sea level, the view is immense; sweeping over one thousand square miles, comprising the entire valley of the Connecticut below Mount Holyoke as far as the Haddam hills, the largest valley in New England. This view is checkered over with cities, towns, villages, farms, and farm houses. The eastern horizon line, commencing in the northeast, east of the Ware Valley, in Massachusetts, continues unbroken for more than eighty miles, ending in the heights below Middletown, Connecticut, the nearest point in this line being twenty-five miles distant. The city of Springfield, its churches and prominent buildings, are in full view. Prominently so are the cities of Rockville and Hartford, in Connecticut. By aid of the powerful telescope at the tower, even the time on the Armory clock at Springfield is, under favorable conditions, told. More than one hundred churches can be counted, while at least seventy-five cities, towns, and villages in Massachusetts and Connecticut can be seen.

During the season thousands of people visit the Tower. They come in family and society reunions and Sunday-school excursions. The expense by railroad is slight. Trains stop at Tower Station for passengers holding Tower excursion tickets. The majority prefer to walk the short distance to the tower, but if desired anyone can be taken up in the mountain wagon for a small fare. Connected with the Tower is a large, fine pavilion, fifty by seventy feet, finished up in Carolina and Virginia pine, furnished with all kinds of chairs, settees, seats, and tables, a piano, a telescope, with attendant to point out places of interest; Claude Lorraine

"SATAN'S KINGDOM," NEAR NEW HARTFORD

field and colored glasses, ice water, marble wash bowls, and running water. Refreshments at reasonable prices can be had, or accommodations cheerfully furnished without extra expense to those choosing to bring their own. There is also a good bowling alley, a large, smooth floor for dancing, while near by is a fine grove supplied with out-door seats and tables for large parties, swings, croquet, quoits, and see-saw. In the village, boats, for a row on Farmington River, can be had; also a ball ground.

Excursion tickets, including Tower, are sold at the principal stations on P., R., & N. E. R. R., and special rates made to Sunday-school excursions.

BARTLETT'S TOWER, TARIFFVILLE.

About four miles distant is Old Newgate Prison and an old copper mine operated by English parties two hundred years ago, and for fifty years the prison was used as the only State Prison of Connecticut. Here General Washington sent desperate prisoners during the War of the Revolution. It is a place of great historic interest, and visited by thousands at the present day. Parties are taken from the Tower; round trip for conveyance, 50 cents.

THE GORGE AT TARIFFVILLE.

Have you seen the stream go down
Through the gorge below the town;
Through the chasm which the pent
   Waters of many fountains,
In their mighty passage rent
   Through the mountains?

Many centuries ago,
   Countless springs and myriad rills,
Poured the laughing, rippling flow
   Of their waters from the hills,
Into this vast basin, bound
By the circling hills around;
And they formed a shallow pool,
Limpid, shadowy, and cool,
But the pool no outlet knew,
And its waters spread and grew,
'Till they rolled in swelling deeps
'Neath the overhanging steeps,
Murmuring a loud complaint,
At the adamant restraint.
And while ages rolled away,
Deeper, broader, day by day,
Grew the waters; and they lapped
   On the shelving pebbly shores,
'Till the solid earth was sapped;
And they knocked, knocked, knocked,
At the massive granite doors,
'Till at last the mountain rocked,

TARIFFVILLE.

Groaned and sundered —
And a seething torrent thundered,
　　Through the chasm,
　　In a spasm
　　Of delirious delight ;
Cleaving with stupendous might
　　Mound and boulder,
　　Spur and shoulder ;
Rearing here a precipice,
Delving there a deep abyss,
　　Grinding, crashing,
　　Leaping, dashing,
Sweeping with resistless motion,
Onward, onward to the ocean.

And to-day the waters forge
Through the narrow winding gorge,
In an ever-changing tangle
Of mad waves, that writhe and wrangle
Like unfettered demon legions,
Hurrying from nether regions ;
And they howl, and growl, and roar,
　　As they pour,
Deep anathemas that speak
All the torments of the doomed ;
　　And they shriek,
With demoniacal laughter,
As each billow tumbling after,
　　Is entombed
In a seething gulf, that boils
Where the plunging wave recoils
From a jutting boulder's base ;
And the baffled torrent hisses,
　　As it backward whirls,
　　And hurls
Clouds of foam in stinging kisses,
On the granite's rugged face ;
　　Then it creeps, creeps, creeps,
　　　'Round the edge
　　Of the interposing ledge,
　　And leaps,

WEST NORFOLK.

Like a beast upon its prey,
Down the steeps,
And away
In a lashing, foaming,
Eddying, combing,
Gleaming, glancing,
Gliding, dancing,
Heaven-made
Cascade.

Thus with clangor never ceasing,
With velocity increasing,
And a power that no barrier can oppose ;
On the rushing river goes,
'Till at last,
When the rocky gorge is passed,
Waves and eddies cease their revels,
And along the sandy levels,
Rippling, glancing,
Sing a lullaby entrancing,
And beneath the shadows deep,
Sleep, sleep.

HARTFORD, CONN.

Having reached the eastern terminus of our journey, it
seems proper to devote a few words to this splendid me-
tropolis of the Nutmeg State, not with a view to its advantages as a summer resort,—though be it remembered it has
such advantages,—but to briefly sketch its salient points for
the information of the stranger from the other side of the
Hudson.

Hartford is the capital of the State of Connecticut. It is
a bustling, active city. Its insurance companies and bank-
ing institutions are well known throughout the world, and
the capital invested in them amounts to many millions of
dollars. The manufacturing corporations have a capital of
many millions.

L. of C.

The City of Hartford has about eighty miles of streets, over which many bicycles carry their riders daily. The public buildings, and those of many of the private corporations, are both elegant and substantial. The State House cost $3,100,000, and stands conspicuously on a hill in Bushnell Park in the center of the city, and its gilded dome can be seen many miles away.

The area of Hartford is about ten miles, and its population about fifty-five thousand. It was settled in 1635, and was then called Newtown. In 1637 it was named Hartford. The Dutch built a fort there in 1633, but it passed into English hands in 1654. The first code of laws was drawn up in 1650. In 1687, Sir Edmund Andros came to Hartford while the assembly was in session and demanded the charter, but it was concealed in the famous Charter Oak by Capt. Joseph Wadsworth, and remained hidden until 1689. The original charter is still in existence, and is preserved among the valuable relics in the capitol building. The historic tree survived until 1856. The city was incorporated in 1784, and in 1885 became the sole capital of the State of Connecticut.

HAMPTON, CONN.— N. Y. & N. E. R. R.

LUCIUS WHITAKER—White Stones Hotel. One and one-half miles. Accommodates 60. Adults, $8 to $10; children, half price. Transients, $1.50 to $2 per day. House is located on one of the highest and most sightly points in the State, affording beautiful scenery. Delightful drives in surrounding country. Healthful and invigorating atmosphere and pure water. Fishing and boating in lakes near by. For references and further particulars write proprietor.

CABIN WAY.

Hudson River Day Line. Connecting at Rhinecliff with Steamboat Express for all points on the route.

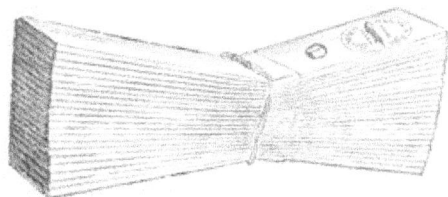

National Blank Book Co.,

HOLYOKE, MASS.

———

An Enjoyable Day's Outing.

Over River, Mountain, and Sound.

320 miles through the grandest scenery in America.

A special day trip from New York has been arranged for during June, July, and August.

Take the Day Line up the Hudson, passing all the historical points of interest, changing at Rhinecliff at 2.10 P. M. to the Steamboat Express train, which will convey the excursionist through valley and over mountains, along lakes and streams, forming one of the most picturesque routes to be found on this continent, arriving at Hartford at 6.40 P. M., leaving at 7.10, 7.40 or 10.05 P. M., via New York, New Haven & Hartford R. R. ; one hour brings you to New Haven, where a change is made to the swift and elegant steamers of the New Haven & New York Line, arriving in New York the following morning.

Round trip tickets on sale at Day Line offices.   Price, $5.00. Three days' stop-over will be granted if desired at any resort. Those wishing to reach New York same evening may exchange tickets at Philadelphia, Reading & New England station, Hartford, for all-rail tickets via New York, New Haven & Hartford R. R., upon payment of 50 cents additional, reaching New York same evening at 10 P. M.

1851. 1894.

THE

Phœnix Mutual Life Ins. Co.,

OF HARTFORD, CONN.,

(ORGANIZED IN 1851.)

OFFERS ALL FORMS OF ENDOWMENT AND LIFE PLANS
FOR LIFE INSURANCE AT LOWEST RATES

DIVIDENDS ANNUALLY.

Cash, Loan, Paid-up, and Extended Insurance values
endorsed on policy yearly.

Highest rate of Interest earned on its Assets.

High Dividends to Policy-Holders.

INCONTESTABLE.

NON-FORFEITABLE. NO RESTRICTIONS.

Send your name and age and full particulars will be
returned to you by mail.

JONATHAN B. BUNCE, *President.* CHARLES H. LAWRENCE, *Secretary.*
JOHN M. HOLCOMBE, *Vice-Pres't.* ARCHIBALD A. WELCH, *Actuary.*

LITCHFIELD.

HILLS

1894